D0269824

The Life of Plants

Plant Products

Richard & Louise Spilsbury

Heinemann
LIBRARY

www.heinemann.co.uk
Visit our website to find out more information about **Heinemann Library** books.

To order:
☎ Phone 44 (0) 1865 888066
▤ Send a fax to 44 (0) 1865 314091
💻 Visit the Heinemann Bookshop at www.heinemann.co.uk to browse our catalogue and order online.

First published in Great Britain by Heinemann Library,

Halley Court, Jordan Hill, Oxford OX2 8EJ

a division of Harcourt Education

Heinemann is a registered trademark of Harcourt Education Ltd.

© Harcourt Education Ltd 2002

The moral right of the proprietor has been asserted.

Designed by Macwiz

Illustrated by Jeff Edwards

Originated by Ambassador Litho Ltd

Printed by Wing King Tong, Hong Kong

ISBN 0 431 11885 X (hardback)

06 05 04 03 02

10 9 8 7 6 5 4 3 2 1

British Library Cataloguing in Publication Data

Spilsbury, Louise
      Plant products. - (Life of plants)
      1. Plant products - Juvenile literature
      I. Title II. Spilsbury, Richard, 1963-
      581.6'3

Acknowledgements

The Publishers would like to thank the following for permission to reproduce photographs:
Christine Osbourne: p28; Corbis: pp5, 18, 21, 24, 26, 32, 33, 34, 35, 36, 37, 39; Gareth Boden: p14;
Holt Studios: pp6, 7, 8, 9, 10, 11, 12, 13, 15, 17, 19, 22, 23, 27, 31, 38; Oxford Scientific Films: p16;
Peter Spilsbury: p29a, 29b; Photodisc: p19b; Science Photo Library: p25, Philippe Plailly/Eurelios p20

Cover photograph reproduced with permission of Tudor Photography

Our thanks to Andrew Solway for his comments in the preparation of this book.

Every effort has been made to contact copyright holders of any material reproduced in this book. Any omissions will be rectified in subsequent printings if notice is given to the Publisher.

Contents

Any words appearing in the text in bold, **like this**, are explained in the glossary.

A plant may be called different things in different countries, so every type of plant has a Latin name that can be recognized anywhere in the world. Latin names are made of two words – the first is the genus (general group) a plant belongs to and the second is its species (specific) name. Latin plant names are given in brackets throughout this book.

Plants for life!

Plants are the key to all life on Earth. Everything that each animal (including you!) does – breathing, moving, eating and even sleeping – requires **energy**. We get energy from our food and all of the food we eat either comes from plants or relies on plants for its own food.

Plant producers

Plants are unique among living things because they can make their own food. For that reason we call them producers. In the process called **photosynthesis**, plants use the energy from sunlight to turn **carbon dioxide** from the air and water from the soil into a kind of sugar, the food that gives them energy to live and grow.

Animal consumers

Animals cannot make their own food. They are consumers – they consume (eat) plants or animals that eat plants. For example, when we eat **fruit** and vegetables, we take in the nourishment locked up in these plant parts and use it to make the energy we need. When we eat beef or drink milk, we are getting the plant's energy second-hand – after the cow that ate grass plants has taken it in!

▶ **The only source of energy available to life on Earth is the Sun, so all food chains, like this one, start with plants because only plants can convert sunlight into sugars.**

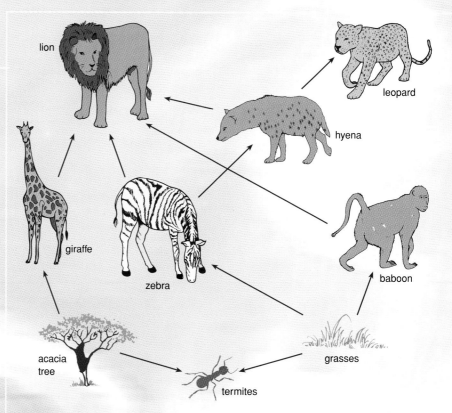

lion

leopard

hyena

giraffe

zebra

baboon

acacia tree

grasses

termites

The air that we breathe

When plants make their own food by photosynthesis, people benefit in other ways. During photosynthesis, plants release **oxygen** into the air. Oxygen is a vital gas for us – we need to breathe in oxygen to carry out **respiration**. Respiration is the way living things get energy from their food. During respiration we release a gas called carbon dioxide. If the levels of carbon dioxide in the air were much higher, it would be poisonous to us. By absorbing (taking in) carbon dioxide to make their food, plants help to keep our air healthy.

That is why the trees that line city streets and fill green parks are so important to the health of people living in towns and cities. Tree leaves trap carbon dioxide and they are particularly good at removing the tiny sooty bits poured into the air from car exhausts. This type of air **pollution** is a real problem for people who have breathing difficulties, such as **asthma**.

▼ Trees and other plants not only make our streets look more attractive, they act like a city's lungs, cleaning the air so people can breathe more easily.

Fruit

In science, a **fruit** is defined as the part of a plant that contains its **seeds**. Some fruits, such as oranges or blackberries, contain many seeds. Others, like grapes, have one or two seeds inside each juicy fruit. In apples, seeds grow inside a core within the fruit. Strawberries are unusual because their seeds grow in the pips on the outside of the fleshy fruit.

Fruit plants

The fruits we eat grow on different kinds of plants. Apples, cherries, plums and oranges grow on trees. Blueberries, gooseberries and blackcurrants grow on bushy plants. Grapes grow on climbing **stems** that wrap around supports to grow tall. Strawberries grow on small plants close to the ground. Banana plants have long leaves that grow from an underground stem.

How do we get seedless grapes?

If fruits hold seeds, why can we buy seedless grapes? Grapes are grown from **cuttings**. The fruit grower cuts a piece of stem from an adult plant and grows it into a new plant identical to the first. At some time in the past an odd grape plant must have grown without seeds. These sold well, so farmers produced more seedless grapes by growing new plants from cuttings of this one.

◄ The bases of the leaves on a banana plant grow so tightly together they look like a tree trunk.

Where do fruits grow?

Some fruits grow best in countries with a **temperate** climate – these are countries which have a cold season every year. The most successful temperate fruits are apples, pears, plums, cherries, blueberries, strawberries and grapes. Citrus fruits, such as oranges, lemons and grapefruit, need warm temperatures most of the year. Some fruits, such as bananas, pineapples, mangoes, papayas and guavas, can only grow in the **tropics**.

Eating fruit

Many fruits taste sweet because they are designed to tempt animals to eat them and so help disperse the plant's seeds. The natural sugars in fruit are essential for animals like us. Our bodies can turn them into **energy** easily and quickly.

Fruit is also the best source of **vitamin** C you can eat. This vital vitamin helps to keep your blood and teeth healthy, heals your wounds and helps to protect you against colds. Fruit also contains fibre. As fibre passes through your body, it keeps your digestive system clean and healthy.

Liquid gold – olive oil

The olive **oil** we use for cooking and to make salad dressings comes from olives, which are fruits of the olive plant. Around 4 to 5 kg of olives are crushed to make just 1 litre of olive oil.

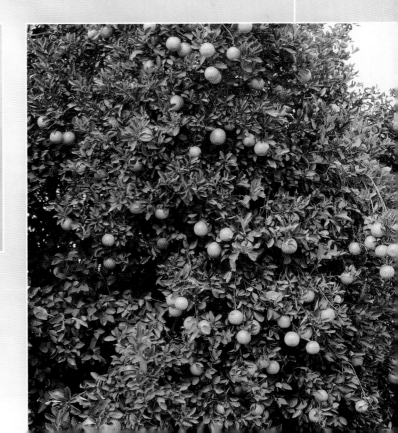

▶ **Oranges are one of the world's most popular fruits. Most of the oranges in this orchard in Florida, USA, will be processed into fruit juice.**

Vegetables

◄ Some of the vegetables we buy may be grown locally; others may be **imported** from countries far away.

Fruit or vegetable?

Some of the plant parts you see in the vegetable section of your supermarket are actually **fruits**. We think of tomatoes, peppers and aubergines as vegetables because we cook them in savoury dishes like stews and casseroles, but in scientific terms they are fruits. A fruit is the part of the plant that grows around its **seeds**. This confusion happens the other way round too – we think of rhubarb as a fruit because we cook it in desserts, but it is the leaf stalk of a plant, so it is really a vegetable!

Peas, carrots, potatoes, broccoli, aubergines, celery – the list of vegetables we eat is seemingly endless. We eat some vegetables fresh; others we buy tinned or frozen. Some we eat raw; others we always cook first. Vegetables are eaten in hundreds of different ways and are a vital part of people's diets all over the world.

What is a vegetable

A vegetable is a plant that is eaten whole or in part, raw or cooked, usually with a main meal or in a salad, but not usually as a dessert. In some cases we eat the underground parts of the plant – carrots are a kind of **root**, potatoes are **tubers** and onions are **bulbs**.

Some vegetables are the tasty leaves of different plants, such as watercress, spinach and chard. Celery sticks are leaf stalks, and asparagus and bamboo shoots are parts of **stems**. We also eat flowers, such as broccoli, and buds, such as brussel sprouts.

Good for you!

Plants contain **energy**, which they make from **photosynthesis**, but they also take up **nutrients** from the soil (through their roots). When we eat plant parts, we take in these nutrients. Fresh vegetables contain nutrients such as **vitamin** C. They also give us **minerals** such as **calcium** and **iron**, which our bodies need to grow strong and healthy. Vegetables also contain **carbohydrates**, one of the body's main sources of energy.

Vegetables from the sea!

Most of us eat sea vegetables every day, though we don't know it! Manufacturers use them as thickeners in products such as ice cream, salad dressings and even toothpaste. You can also eat sea vegetables in meals. Thin, dry sheets of nori seaweed (*Porphyra lanceolata*) are used in Japanese soups and to wrap sushi (little parcels of rice and fish). In the UK, young shoots of the seashore samphire plant (*Crithmum maritimum*) are eaten as a side vegetable.

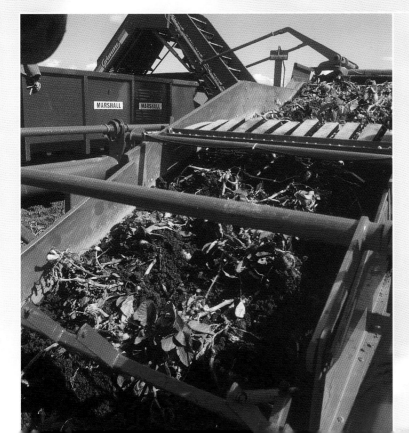

◄ Potatoes being harvested. Potatoes are the potato plant's underground food store. They are full of carbohydrates, which means they are a kind of food that gives us lots of energy.

Nuts and seeds

Nuts are **seeds** covered with a hard shell. Most are the seeds of trees. The bit we eat, which we often call the nut, is actually the kernel, the seed inside the shell. Nuts and other seeds are the parts that can grow into new plants. Seeds contain food that the new plant can use to make the **energy** it needs for its first days of growth. This food store is rich in **protein** and **fat**, making it a useful source of goodness for us too.

You can buy nuts in their shell or with shells removed. Nuts can be eaten in many ways – whole, flaked or ground, or turned into nut butters. Many nuts are roasted and eaten as snacks, or added to savoury meals and sweet foods like puddings, cakes and biscuits.

Peanuts – peas or nuts?

Did you know that the peanut is more closely related to peas than nuts? Like pea plants, the peanut plant is a **legume** that protects its seeds inside a **pod**. The unusual thing about peanut pods is that they grow under the ground. That is why they are often called 'groundnuts'. **Stalks** grow out of the centre of the plant's dead flower heads into the ground. Two seeds (the peanuts) grow inside the tip of each stalk, and the stalks develop into hard pods.

Kinds of nuts

The biggest nut in the world is the coconut. You can eat the white flesh inside the brown husky shell fresh or dried. Almond nuts are one of the most popular nuts. In fact, coconuts and almonds are really the 'stones' of **fruits**! The coconut has a fibrous outer fruit; the almond a leathery one.

▲ Almonds are not true nuts. They are really the stones inside the fruit of the almond tree.

Pecan nuts are true nuts. They are enclosed in a thick green husk that splits open when ripe. Chestnuts grow inside spiny seed cases. White, bean-shaped cashew nuts are unusual because they grow in shells that dangle from the end of fruit-like parts known as cashew apples.

Seed surprises

As well as nuts we eat many other kinds of seeds, from tiny white sesame seeds to flat green pumpkin seeds. Many seeds are crushed to remove their **oils**. Oils from linseeds and sunflower seeds are used for cooking oil and in margarine. Some, like sunflower and pumpkin seeds, are roasted in oil and salt to make a snack food.

Some seeds, such as sesame seeds, have a great variety of uses in cooking. Whole sesame seeds decorate cakes and breads. Sesame oil is used in many oriental dishes. Sesame seed paste, called tahini, is used in a savoury spread called hummus. Sesame seeds are also crushed with sugar to make a sweet called halva.

▲ A sunflower head is actually made up of many tiny individual flowers. A seed can develop from every one.

11

Cereals

If someone told you that they eat grass for breakfast, you would probably think they were a little crazy. Yet you probably do just the same thing yourself! Most of the breakfast cereals we tuck into each morning are made from the **seeds** of different kinds of grass plants.

Cereals are members of the grass **family** of plants. The seeds of cereal plants are called grains and are used to make many of the world's most useful foods. Some of the most important cereals include wheat, maize (corn), rice, rye, oats, barley and millet. Some cereal grains, such as rice, are eaten much as they come off the plant. Some, such as wheat, are ground (crushed) into flour, which in turn can be used to make bread, pasta or puddings. Corn, rice and wheat grains are **processed** to make breakfast cereals.

▲ When wheat plants are fully grown, they are around 1.5 m tall and golden-brown.

Wheat wonders

Wheat is the most important food for more than a third of the people in the world. Wheat plants cover more of the Earth's surface than any other food crop. In one year the world's farmers grow enough to fill a train stretching around the world more than 20 times!

Rice

Rice is a staple (very important food) for more than half the people of the world. People in Asia have grown rice for food for over 5000 years. Some rice is still grown on terraces (hilly patches surrounded by mud walls to keep water in) built around 2000 years ago. Rice is a unique kind of cereal crop because it is the only one that grows with its roots under water.

▲ Rice seedlings are planted in paddy fields that are flooded with water.

Cereal plants

Cereal plants are efficient food producers because they grow and make seeds quickly. Lots of plants can be grown closely together so that one field of plants can produce a large amount of grain. The grains (seeds) we eat come from a cluster of flowers at the top of the cereal plant, called a spikelet. Grass plants are **wind-pollinated**, so they do not need colourful flowers to attract insects for **pollination**. Instead, they have green leaf-like scales around the flower parts that will grow the seeds.

Good for you!

Inside a seed there is a tiny **embryo**, but most of the space is taken up with stored food. The food is there to make **energy** for the embryo to **germinate**. When we eat seeds, we get the benefit of this valuable food store. Grass seeds such as corn, wheat, rice and rye are nutritious (very good for you) because they store **proteins** and **carbohydrates**, which give you energy and keep you healthy.

Beans and peas

Beans and peas are kinds of **seeds**. They belong to a large **family** of plants called **legumes** – these are plants that grow their seeds in cases, called **pods**. Beans and peas contain **vitamins** and a lot of **protein**.

Some beans are picked before they are fully developed and eaten fresh. You can cook and eat the pods of some, such as runner beans (*Phaseolus coccineus*), with the seeds. Other beans, such as broad beans (*Vicia faba*), are removed from the pods first. Some beans are left to develop fully on the plant before being picked. These are often called dry beans because they are hard and can be stored for a long time. You have to soak dry beans, such as kidney beans (*Phaseolus vulgaris*), before cooking them.

▲▼ There are many different kinds of beans of all shapes and sizes, ranging from large deep-red kidney beans, to tiny green mung beans (*Vigna mungo*).

Take a trip to Beantown!

The story of baked beans starts in the 17th century in the city of Boston, USA. Puritans living there were people with strong religious beliefs, one of which was that it was wrong to cook on Sundays. So, many families prepared baked beans on Saturdays, ready for Sunday supper. These were so popular that for a while Boston was known as 'Beantown'! Today baked beans are a favourite food in many countries.

Ways of growing

Some legume plants grow as bushes, but many grow as climbing plants, like peas. Most bean plants climb by twisting their main **stems** around another plant's stem for support. Pea plants have softer stems. They climb using tendrils – long, thin leaflets that grow from the leaves. These twist around other stems or leaves of tall grasses to hold the plant up to the light.

There are many different kinds of peas, including black-eyed peas, chick peas and sugarsnap peas. Some have lots of seeds in a single pod, while others have very few – chick peas only have one or two peas per pod. When you eat sugarsnap peas you eat the pods as well as the peas inside. The most common type of pea is the green or garden pea, the kind we eat as a vegetable with a main meal.

The world's most useful bean?

At less than a metre tall with small flowers and pods, the soya-bean plant may not look very special, but its beans are incredibly versatile. You may know about bean curd, soy sauce and miso but many other things we eat contain parts of soya beans, including many **processed** foods such as sweets, baby foods, sausages and burgers. Soya beans are also used to make **vegetarian** products, which are chemically treated to look and taste like meat. Soya beans can even be used to make plastic bags that are **biodegradable**, rotting away in soil after they have been thrown away.

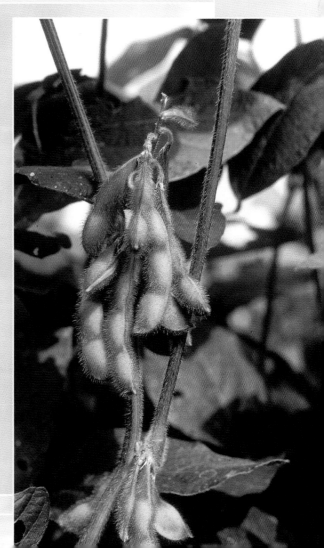

Drinks

People have made drinks from plants for thousands of years. You can take some drinks straight from the plant, such as the 'milk' in a coconut. **Fruits** such as orange, apple and pineapple are pressed to make fruit juices, or blended with yoghurt or ice cream to make smoothies or shakes. Different parts of plants are used to add flavour to fizzy drinks, such as lemon juice in lemonade.

▲ Tea bushes grow in large areas called plantations. Pickers select the younger leaves, as they give the best flavour.

Tea

Around half the people in the world drink tea. Most tea is made from the leaf tips of **evergreen** camellia bushes, which grow mainly on high, wet hills in Asia. The leaves are picked, dried and crushed, and people then soak them in boiling water to release their flavour. Different varieties of tea plants produce teas of different tastes. Sometimes fruits and other plant parts are added to create new flavours. The leaves of different plants such as peppermint and chamomile are used to make herbal teas.

The cow tree?

In parts of South America there is a tree that people can drink from. The cow- or milk-tree produces lots of sweet, white **sap** that oozes out from under its **bark** if it is cut. This creamy liquid tastes a bit like cow's milk!

Drinking chocolate

The first people to enjoy chocolate drinks were the Mayans, who lived in Central America 1400 years ago. They made a spicy drink by mixing water and chilli pepper with the roasted, crushed seeds of the cacao tree. Today we use cacao seeds to make sweet chocolate drinks. The seeds are ground up to make a dark liquid. All seeds contain **fat** and the fat (cocoa butter) in this liquid is removed to make cocoa powder. This can be mixed with sugar and milk to make drinking chocolate. If the cocoa liquid is mixed with sugar and extra cocoa butter, solid chocolate is the result!

▲ Cacao fruits (**pods**) grow out of the stem of a tropical tree. They each contain 20 to 30 seeds. When the pods are ripe, the farmers split them open with long knives and scoop out the seeds.

Coffee

Coffee is made from coffee beans. Although they are called beans, they are really the **seeds** of berries that grow on a type of small tree found in hot, **humid** parts of the world. The berries are picked from the plant when they are ripe, then dried or soaked to remove their flesh. The two hard seeds inside are then roasted to release their flavour and smell. Coffee is made by grinding the roasted beans and mixing them with hot water. When this liquid has been strained, the coffee is ready to drink.

Adding flavour

We use lots of different plant parts to add flavour and colour to our food, from the sugar we add to drinking chocolate, the basil leaves we chop into sauces and the pepper we grind into soup. People have been using herbs and spices to add flavour (and to disguise the taste of meat that was less than fresh) for thousands of years.

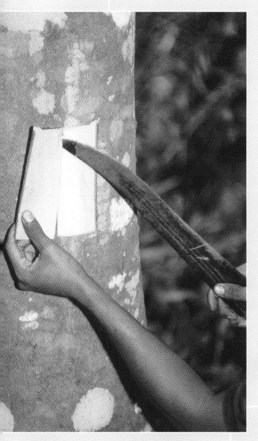

▲ Cinnamon is made from the **bark** of a tree that grows in India and Sri Lanka. The cinnamon sticks we buy are pieces of thin bark, cut from a young tree, which have curled up as they dried.

Spices

Spices come from a variety of different plant parts. Peppercorns are the sun-dried berries of the pepper vine. They are usually crushed or powdered before being added to food. Cloves are the dried **buds** of a tropical tree. Tangy-tasting ginger is the underground **stem** of another tropical plant. You can use ginger fresh (peeled), dried or ground to add flavour to savoury meals or cakes and puddings. Chillies are spicy fruits, full of **seeds**. They are eaten fresh (in very small quantities) or dried to make chilli powder. The nutmeg tree provides us with two different spices. Nutmeg is the tree's seed. Mace is the fleshy network that surrounds the seeds. Both are ground and used in sweet and savoury foods.

Herbs

Most herbs are the leaves or stems of certain plants that have distinctive flavours. Herbs can either be eaten fresh or they can be dried, crushed into a powder and stored in airtight containers, so that they last longer. People use herbs to add flavour to savoury dishes. For example, basil or oregano leaves taste good in tomato sauces. Chive **stalks** are used in salads or egg dishes. Mint leaves are used in sauces. Some herbs, such as parsley, are a good source of **vitamins** A and C, but you need to eat a lot of it to get the benefits of these.

Many herbs, such as mint, sage, oregano and thyme, grow as small, bright green leaves on low-growing bushes. Dill plants are taller than many herb plants and their leaves are long and feathery. Most herbs are **perennial** plants, which live and flower for several years.

▶ Sugar cane.

▲ Sugar beet plants.

Sweet facts – sugar

Most of the sugar we use to sweeten our food and drinks comes from two very different kinds of plants – sugar cane and sugar beet. Sugar cane is a kind of tall grass that grows in the **tropics** and sugar is made from its stems. The sugar beet plant grows in **temperate** areas of the world and sugar is made from its thickened **roots**. The sugar crystals extracted from these very different plants look and taste just the same!

Medicines

People discovered that plants could be used to treat illness thousands of years ago. They would have worked out which plants could help with different complaints by trial and error – trying each one out until they found one that worked. Gradually people passed on their discoveries by word of mouth and later wrote them down. Many plants were even named according to the medicinal properties they have. Lungwort is used to help with some breathing problems and was named after the part of the body used for breathing – the lungs.

Today many of the medicines we use are made from artificial (laboratory-made) chemicals, but most of the world's population use plant medicines. Some may be used for fairly minor problems. For example, people breathe in **oil** from eucalyptus leaves to clear blocked noses when they have a cold. Other plants may be used to treat more serious conditions. Foxgloves are tall spikes of purple flowers. Their leaves contain a poison called digitalis, which deters small animals from eating them. Scientists use this poison to make a drug that helps the human heart beat more slowly and strongly. Some people with heart problems say they owe their lives to this common plant.

▶ Some chemicals produced by plants, like the anti-cancer drug Taxol, made from the Pacific yew (*Taxus brevifolia*), can successfully treat some illnesses.

Other medicinal plants

Another very poisonous plant that can be used to our advantage is belladonna, also known as deadly nightshade. A drug called atropine is made from the berries of the belladonna plant. It is used to dilate (widen) the pupils of the eyes when they are being checked or operated on, and also to treat stomach problems.

Other medicines come from the **stems**, **roots** or **bark** of plants. The **sap** from the stem of an opium poppy is used to make tablets such as codeine, which reduce the discomfort of headaches or other pains. The root of ginseng, a plant related to ivy, has been used in China for thousands of years. The root is ground to a powder and many people across the world say that it has helped them recover from illness, relieved headaches and tiredness, among other problems. It is the bark of the cinchona tree of South America that is used to make quinine, a treatment for malaria, one of the most terrible diseases in the world today.

▶ **Records suggest that in China people had identified more than 350 plants that could be used to make medicines as much as 5000 years ago! Recent studies have found that today 75–80 per cent of the world's population still use plant medicines.**

Perfumes and essential oils

Many of the scents we use in perfumes, bath oils, shampoos and creams come from plants. Plant scents are stored in the form of **oils**, known as essential oils. Plants contain oils for a number of reasons. Some plants use sweet scents to attract insects or other animals to help them **pollinate** their flowers. Some plants use strong-smelling scents for the opposite reason – to repel animals that might want to eat them. In some cases, the oils protect the plant from disease, stopping them from becoming infected by germs that may invade through a damaged **stem**.

Aromatherapy

Aromatherapy is the use of plant oils to treat people's problems and make them feel better. Oils may be heated so their scent fills the air, added to bath water or used on the skin. The different oils help people in different ways. For example, lavender is a calming scent and the oil helps to heal burns. Orange relaxes and refreshes you. Rosemary can help with breathing problems.

Tea tree tales

You don't make tea from the tea trees (*Leptospermum*) of Australia! Oil extracted from the leaves is one of nature's finest **antiseptics**, used by native Aborigine tribes to fight **infections** for thousands of years. Explorer Captain Cook gave the tea tree its English name in 1768. He stewed its leaves in hot water (like tea) for his crew to drink to prevent a disease called scurvy.

► **Flowers and leaves of the tea tree plant.**

Plants make their scents in different parts. A rose has scented oil in its **petals**, the eucalyptus tree has it in its leaves, cinnamon in its **bark**, garlic in **bulbs**, and sandalwood trees in the heart of the **trunk**. Oranges make three slightly different scented oils in their flowers, leaves and rind.

Extracting oils

Most oils are extracted (taken out) using steam. When steam is forced through plant parts, the heat makes the droplets of oil and water inside the plant **evaporate** (turn into a gas, called **vapour**). The vapour is collected and cooled so it turns back into liquid oil and water. Oils from **citrus fruits**, such as orange, are extracted by 'cold pressing'. The rind is removed, ground up and pressed to squeeze out the oils. Some perfumes are expensive because it takes a lot of plant material to make a little oil. To make one litre of rose oil it takes the flowers of 100,000 roses!

Plant power – fuel from plants

We rely on fuel for almost everything we do. We use fuel to cook our food, heat and light our homes, and power our cars and computers. At one time, wood was the world's main source of fuel. In many countries wood is still the most important fuel – around nine out of ten people in developing countries rely on burning wood for heating and cooking. Wood is the most obvious fuel to come from plants, but did you know that coal, oil and natural gas also come from plants?

▲ The coal being dug from this mine in Russia today formed from plants that died millions of years ago.

Fossil fuels

Coal, oil and gas are often called 'fossil fuels'. Fossils are the remains of dead plants (and animals) that lived around 300 million years ago. As they rotted away and broke down, the **energy** inside some of them became stored in another form. Take the story of coal. Ancient plants trapped the sun's energy to make their food by **photosynthesis**, just as plants do today. When they died and their remains broke up in the soil, some of that energy was buried with them. In swampy areas plants decay very slowly, and dead, rotting plants piled up and squashed together to form **peat**, which can be burnt.

Gradually layers of clay, sand and stones got washed on top of the peat. Over millions of years the weight of these layers squashed the peat so much that it became hard, and turned into coal. Oil and gas were created in much the same way, but in areas that were not swampy. Heat, **bacteria** and the weight of layers of rock above turned the remains into oil or gas, trapped below ground.

When we burn oil, gas and coal we release the stored energy as heat. The heat can be used to make steam to turn turbines to make electricity. Useful though they are, there is only a limited amount of fossil fuels, and they will eventually run out.

New plant fuels

Fossil fuels take millions of years to form, so once they are gone they cannot be used again. The oil from which we get petrol will run out one day, so scientists are looking for alternatives to power our cars.

▲ This technician is working at a factory where sugar juices are transformed into ethanol.

Plants such as sugar cane, cassava and corn are loaded with sugars. Plant sugars can be collected and turned into an alcohol, called **ethanol**, which can be used as a fuel. A number of buses in Sweden and cars in Brazil already run on sugarcane alcohol. There has also been research into using plant oils, from vegetables or beans, such as the soya bean, as fuels.

Building

Around the world many different plants are used for building. Some cottages still have thatched roofs made from straw, the dried **stalks** of a grass plant. In parts of the Middle East people build homes and boats from reeds. In Indonesia some roofs are made from banana leaves. The bamboo plant is used for many houses and bridges in parts of Asia. However, the plant most used for building is the tree.

Wood

In order to support their height and the weight of their leaf-laden branches, trees have incredibly strong **stems** called **trunks**. As a tree grows taller, its trunk grows wider. The area of growth is just under the **bark**. The old wood inside the trunk is dead and as it dries up it becomes hard and tough.

Wood is used in many building projects, in frames for windows and supporting walls for houses, and to make sheds, tools, furniture and boats. It is useful because it is hard and strong. Also, it can be cut or carved into many, and often intricate, shapes; it is strong but also springy; it does not rust as many metals do; and if it is properly looked after, wood can last for hundreds of years.

◄ **Bamboo is a kind of grass, which has tough woody stalks, making it an ideal building material. Bamboo scaffolding is used for almost all building and repair jobs in Hong Kong.**

From tree to timber

Timber is the word used to describe 'useful wood'. People usually divide timber into **softwoods** and **hardwoods**. Softwoods come from **coniferous** trees such as spruce or pine. Hardwoods are more expensive because they come from slower growing **broad-leaved** trees, such as oak.

In the forest, power saws are used to fell (cut down) trees and slice off their branches. Because the tree was alive when it was cut down, the trunk still contains a lot of **sap** and is quite wet inside. If cut into planks when wet, the pieces would shrink and warp (bend) as they dried out. Logs are usually dried out (seasoned) first, either in air or in warm rooms, to speed up the process. Then the bark is ripped off and the seasoned timber is sliced into planks or boards, ready to be used for building work.

Wood cheats

Big planks of wood can be expensive, so manufacturers make cheaper substitutes. Plywood and blockboard are made by sticking lots of thin sheets of wood together. Chipboard and fibreboard are made out of tiny chippings of wood or sawdust mixed with glue, all squashed together to form large boards. Veneers are thin sheets of expensive wood that cover chipboard so it looks like solid wood.

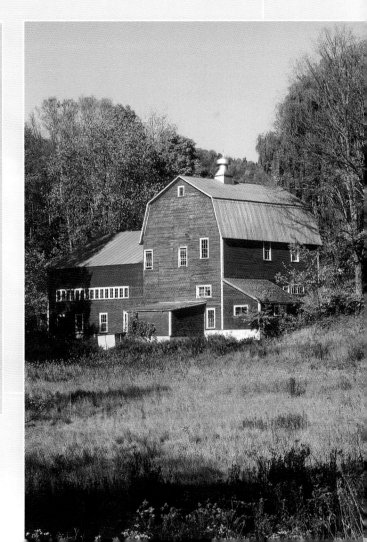

▶ This house is made from timber. The wooden frame is covered in overlapping planks.

In the home

If you look around your home, you may be able to see lots of things made from plants, from wooden tables to woven baskets. Different plant materials are suitable for different objects. The wood used to make a table is chosen for its strength and also for the way it looks. Willow or bamboo **stems** are used to make baskets because they are soft enough to weave together, but harden as they dry.

Hardwoods

Some **hardwoods** used for furniture, such as mahogany and teak, grow in **rainforests**. So many have been cut down in the past that they are now very rare. Hardwoods grow very slowly, so it is not easy to replace them. Today, laws protect many of the hardwood forests that remain.

Wood colours and grains

The **timber** you get from each tree is different, both in colour and pattern (grain). When a **trunk** is cut down its length to make planks for furniture, the tree's **annual rings** show up as attractive, curling lines called grains. Walnut wood has a particularly attractive grain, cherry wood is reddish like its fruit, mahogany is a very rich, dark brown wood and oak is very tough but has an attractive grain.

► A rainforest in Indonesia.

Under foot

There are many plant materials that can be used for flooring, including **fibres** such as seagrass, coir, jute and sisal. In the **tropics**, people use strips of coconut palm leaves to make mats. The coconut husk is made up of short, stiff fibres (called coir) that can be woven together to make mats, ropes and brooms.

Sisal (*Agave sisalana*) is another plant grown for its strong fibre. Sisal fibre is obtained from the plant's sword-like leaves, which can grow to 1.5 metres long. The leaves are crushed to squeeze out any soft plant material and juices, and then the coarse fibres are scraped, washed and dried. Sisal is used to make rope, doormats and rugs. Today, sisal is mostly grown in dry regions of Brazil, Tanzania, Angola, Kenya and Madagascar.

▲ **Preparing the coconuts.**

▲ **Coir mats are made from the hairy brown husk of the coconut.**

House plant tips

Most of us also like having live plants in the home! Before choosing a new house plant, look at the room you'll be putting it in. Is it dry or **humid** and how light is it? In the shop, check the plant's label to see what it needs, for example, light and temperature are most important for flowering plants. Does the plant need sunlight through a window or a constant temperature? Some house plants are very particular about soil and **fertilizer** (plant food), so you may need to buy these too.

Clothing and accessories

Take a look at the labels inside your clothes – the chances are that at least one of the things you are wearing started life as a plant! Many clothes and accessories across the world are made from plants.

Fibres and fabrics

Some fabrics are made of **fibres** from plant parts. Plant fibres are useful because they are strong but flexible enough to weave together. Flax fibres come from the **stem** of the flax plant (*Linum Usitatissimum*). They are extracted by soaking and beating the plant, and then woven together to make linen. Panama hats are made of young leaf fibres from the **shoots** of the straw palm (*Carludovica palmata*). Leaves from the raffia palm (*Raphia farinifera*) make raffia, a fibre woven to make baskets and hats.

Amber jewellery

Amber is actually **resin** that seeped from fir and pine trees around 50 million years ago. As it hardened it formed the bronze gemstone used for jewellery today. Some pieces of amber even have insects inside, trapped in time as the oozing resin flowed over them.

Cotton on!

About three out of four people across the world wear cotton clothes. Cotton fabric is light but strong, so cotton clothes, such as jeans, last a long time.

Cotton fibres come from the **pod** of the cotton plant (*Gossypium hirsutum*). The fluffy white fibres grow on the **seeds** inside the pods and there are about 30 seeds inside each pod. When the seeds are ripe, the pods open up to reveal the fibres. Cotton pickers harvest the open pods (called bolls) before the fibres are blown away.

Even the longest cotton fibres are no more than 4 centimetres long. To make long reels of thread a machine twists and spins many fibres together to make one long thread or yarn. Finally, two or more threads are woven together to make sheets of fabric.

▲ The cotton plant grows cotton fibres so that its seeds will be more easily caught by the wind and blown onto new soil where some of them might grow.

Tree silk?

Rayon fabric is sometimes called 'tree silk' because it is made from **cellulose**, a chemical in wood. To make rayon, wood is chemically treated to dissolve the cellulose so that it forms a liquid. It is then forced through tiny holes in a machine to make sticky threads. When these harden they can be woven together to make fabric.

Paper

How many products made of paper or cardboard can you think of? You are reading a book made from paper right now. You could list writing paper, newspapers, magazines and comics, paper wrapping and packing products, greetings cards, currency (money), bathroom and kitchen papers and wallpapers. Paper is a vital part of our everyday lives and it comes from plants.

From plant to page

Most modern papers are mainly made of **cellulose** taken from wood, usually from **softwood** trees such as pines and firs. Around half of the wood pulp used to make paper comes from wood chips – waste woods left over from cutting **timber** for other uses, such as building.

To make paper, **bark** is stripped off the logs and the wood is broken into tiny pieces (cellulose **fibres**) in a big machine. Then the fibres are mixed with chemicals and water to make wood pulp. The wet pulp is poured onto a conveyor (moving) belt that is made of wire mesh. As the belt moves along, water drains through the mesh, leaving the damp paper fibres on the surface.

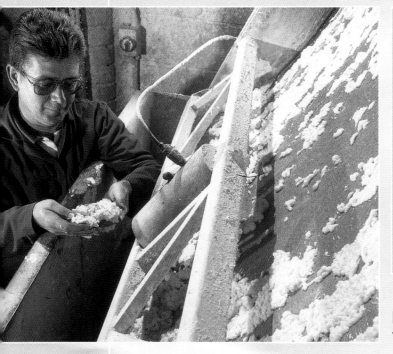

Past papers

People have used some form of paper for thousands of years. In fact, the word 'paper' comes from the Egyptian word papyrus, a type of reed plant from which ancient Egyptians made a kind of writing material. The Chinese invented the first real paper, some time before AD 100.

◄ On a conveyor belt, wet wood pulp already looks a little like the paper it will become.

The conveyor then passes the wet paper fibres through rollers. These squeeze out more water and squash the fibres so they stick together. To completely dry out the paper, the conveyor runs it through hot rollers, and as it comes out dry it is wound onto a giant reel in one endless sheet.

Different kinds of paper

Other fibres such as cotton, linen, hemp and straw are also used to make paper, but these are less common. Different things can also be added to the wood pulp stage to create different kinds of paper. Chemicals give the paper a particular colour or kind of coating (such as a shiny finish). China clay can make the paper stronger. A chemical called 'size' (which is actually **resin**) may be used to coat the paper, so it doesn't become too absorbent. Dyes may be added to colour it.

▼ Many different plant fibres can be used to make paper. This man, who lives in China, is using mulberry pulp.

Waste not, want not – recycling paper

Millions of trees are cut down to make paper, and yet it is easy to recycle paper. When waste paper is soaked in water, it breaks back down into its original fibres. The ink can be washed off and the pulp used to make new paper products. Recycled paper is mostly used to make cardboard, napkins, newspapers and even cereal boxes, but it can be used to make better quality paper too.

Cleaning up

Believe it or not, water by itself is not much use for cleaning. Water has a property called surface tension, which means it runs off surfaces such as your skin. To see how surface tension works, place a drop of water onto a plastic or glass tabletop and watch how it forms a bead shape and does not spread out. This means it takes longer to wet a surface you want to clean. To make water useful for cleaning, we need to add a soap of some kind. When soap is added to water, surface tension reduces, so water spreads out and wets surfaces properly. Soap also attaches itself to any bits of dirt so that when you rinse off the soap, the dirt gets washed away too.

One of the main ingredients of soap is **fat**. Much soap today is made using vegetable **oils** (a kind of fat), such as olive oil, palm oil, sesame oil and soya-bean oil. When the oils are heated with a chemical and salt, a soapy mixture floats to the surface. This is removed and pressed together to form soap.

Soap lilies

One of the most unusual uses for members of the large lily plant **family** is soap. Some Native Americans used the juice of the soap-plant's (*Chlorogalum pomeridianum*) onion-like **bulb** for cleaning – crushed bulbs rubbed on the hands make a soapy lather when rubbed vigorously with water.

◄ The Arcata Marsh sewage system in California, USA. The marshes also make a great **habitat** for wetland birds and animals.

Cleaning up contaminated ground

Plants can also help us clean up soils **contaminated** with toxic (poisonous) metals! Many plants cannot grow on contaminated soils but some, such as Indian mustard, poplars, sunflowers and ferns, can. When planted in contaminated areas, they suck up water containing dissolved toxic metals from the soil through their **roots**. The metals are carried to other plant parts, such as **stems**, shoots and leaves. These parts can be cut and removed, leaving the ground clean.

Plants and sewage

Sewage is the waste-water from household pipes, the stuff that washes down the drains from our kitchens and bathrooms. Many sewage works use tiny **algae** (small plant forms). Algae grow well in sewage because it is a good source of **nutrients** for them. The algae make **oxygen** (during the process of **photosynthesis**), which **bacteria** use to help them break down the waste in the water.

In reed-bed sewage systems, plants are used in another cleansing stage. Marshy wetlands are used or created, where reeds, cattails and bulrushes thrive. As waste-water flows through them, these plants act like a natural sieve. Reed beds take longer to set up, but are much cheaper to run than ordinary sewage works. Money is also saved because no pipes and tanks are required.

Conservation

Conservation means the planned management of the natural world – the **habitats** of the Earth and the plants and animals that live in them. Although plants often require protection themselves, they also play an important role in conservation as they provide food and shelter for a whole variety of other plants and animals.

Countless insects, many too small for us even to see, eat the leaves of plants. Insects and other tiny creatures live on or in tree **bark**. Butterflies and other insects lay their eggs on plant leaves and **stems**. Birds, wild bees, monkeys and squirrels live in holes or build nests in tall trees, to be safe from other animals. Trees also provide homes for other plants. In moist climates, mosses and ferns grow in trees. In the **tropics**, **bromeliads** and orchids live on branches in the sky.

▲ An adult giant panda eats around 20 kg of the tall grass plant, bamboo, each day.

Panda protection

The giant panda is a good example of an animal that is vitally linked to its habitat. The panda is now an endangered species. That means that there are not many pandas left in the world and one day the last may die out. One of the reasons for this is that pandas only eat bamboo and humans are cutting down the bamboo forests where they live.

Erosion control

Erosion is the loss of soil as it is loosened and moved by wind, frost, rain or water. The top layer of soil is particularly important to land, as it is rich in the **nutrients** that plants need to grow. Erosion is an important conservation issue in many countries of the world and plants can help to solve the problem in different ways.

Plants can be used to protect areas of land or other plants by acting as windbreaks. Strong winds can cause real difficulties for farmers, as storms can blow down crops or carry away soil from a field. A row of trees can provide a shield against even the strongest winds.

Roots not only hold plants firmly in the soil, they also hold the soil around the roots. Trees on a hillside can reduce the risk of landslides. Trees, such as willow (*Salix*) and alder (*Alnus*), which grow along riverbanks, develop a tangle of strong roots that hold the soil and reduce the amount of earth washed away from the bank by the moving water. Along sandy shores, the deep roots of marram grasses (*Ammophila arenaria*) prevent sands from shifting, and, as the grasses die and rot, they create a layer of humus (rich plant matter) in which other plants can grow.

◄ Along the coast of the Netherlands, special grasses protect the sand dunes from erosion and the low lands beyond from the stormy North Sea.

Plants for leisure

Plants not only provide us with many of life's necessities, they also give us many of the products we use for fun. Plants are involved in many of our leisure activities, from the grass pitches and fields we play games on, to the canoes and boats we row or sail.

A baseball bat's handle is made from hickory (*Carya*) and ash (*Fraxinus*), two **hardwoods** that have long, solid **fibres** inside. This makes the bat good and strong. The blade (the bit the ball hits) of many cricket bats is made from the strong but flexible wood of a white willow (*Salix alba caerulea*) that grows in India.

Music and art

Some musical instruments, such as guitars and violins, have bodies made from wood. The black keys on some pianos are made from ebony (*Pithecellobium flexicaule*), a very hard and rare black wood that grows in African **rainforests**. Reeds used in the mouthpieces of saxophones and clarinets are cut from bamboo plants.

▲ The rubber used to make wheels and tyres is the **sap** of rubber trees (*Hevea brasiliensis*). It is collected when the **bark** of the tree is cut.

The pencil or charcoal you use for sketching comes from wood from trees. Wood surrounds the lead in your pencils and charcoal is what is left behind after wood has been burnt in a kiln. It can be squeezed together to make charcoal crayons.

Plants for pleasure

Without plants we would not exist. Plants provide us with the air we breathe and the food we eat. They clothe and shelter us. They are used to make drinks that quench our thirst, medicines that heal us and scents that soothe us. Plants are the source of paper used to make the books, newspapers and magazines that inform us. These things are all vitally important to our lives on this planet, but there is one other product of plant life that we have not yet mentioned – the pleasure plants give us as themselves.

People get immense satisfaction and pleasure from looking at plants, breathing in their scents or basking in their colours, walking through woods, and growing their own plants, either for food or to bring colour to their homes and gardens. For many of us plants also mark the passing seasons. We know summer is making way for autumn when the leaves change colour and begin to fall. We know spring warmth will soon replace the chill of winter when the first flowers burst into bloom. Plants not only help to keep us alive, they also make our lives more pleasurable, day after day.

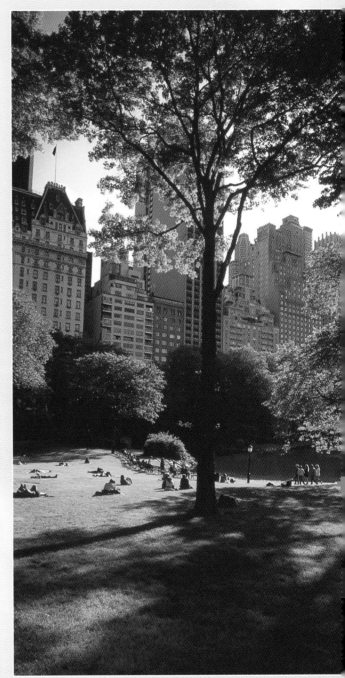

▲ At a time when many of us live in busy cities, parks and gardens provide us with a place to rest or play, while enjoying the colours and scents of the plants within them.

Try it yourself!

Try some of the activities on this page to make some of your own products from plants and also your own food chain.

Create a food chain

Food chains show us how the **organisms** (living things) in a **habitat** depend on each other for food. One food chain, for example, might show a plant that is eaten by a mouse, which in turn is eaten by an owl. Look back at the food chain on page 4 of this book for an example. You can make your own food chains using pictures that you draw, or cut from magazines.

You will need:

- Old magazines with plant and animal pictures
- Scissors
- Pen or pencil
- Glue
- Paper

Choose a top predator, such as a lion, fox or eagle. Find out what animal it eats. Then find out what that animal eats. Keep going, until you get down to a plant. You have found a food chain! Cut out pictures of the animals and plants you have researched to make your own food chain. Stick them onto a sheet of paper and draw lines between them to show how it works. If you cannot find the pictures you want, try drawing your own.

Make your own lemonade!

Using fresh ingredients to make your own food or drinks is a good way to get the most **vitamins** and **nutrients** from your food. This is a simple recipe for a tangy, tasty drink.

You will need:

- 2 tablespoons lemon juice
- 1½ tablespoons lime juice
- 2 tablespoons white caster sugar
- 6 ice cubes
- 2 cups cold water

Squeeze the juice you need from fresh lemons and limes. Pour the juice into a jug. Then add the sugar and stir until dissolved (the sugar becomes part of the juice). Add the ice cubes and water and stir. Pour it into two glasses and serve.

Make a scented pomander

Scented room sprays were not available in the past, so people made their own room fresheners, called pomanders, using natural scents. These were made out of oranges and cloves, and were hung in cupboards. They are still given as nice gifts.

You will need:

- 1 orange
- 20 cloves
- Fork or toothpick
- Muslin, or other lightweight mesh fabric
- Ribbon

Use the fork or toothpick to make holes in the orange. You can make the holes in straight lines or in a pattern. Put a clove into each of the little holes. Then wrap the orange in a square of the muslin. Attach the ribbon to the top of the muslin and make a loop, so the ribbon can be slipped over a rail or coat hanger.

As the orange dries, the fragrance from the **oils** in its rind is released, mixed with the spicy scent of the cloves.

Carrot and apple soup

Most nutritionists (experts on food and health) believe that everyone should eat at least five portions of **fruit** and vegetables every day. This soup contains fruit and vegetables too, making it delicious and good for you. Ask an adult to help you.

You will need:

- 450g carrots
- 1 onion
- 1 potato
- 1 large cooking apple
- 50g butter
- 1 litre vegetable stock
- Salt and pepper to taste

Peel and chop the vegetables into small pieces and cook them in the butter in a large pan for about 5 minutes. Peel and chop the apple and add to the pan. Add the rest of the ingredients. When the soup is boiling (bubbling furiously), put on the lid, turn down the heat a little and let it cook for about 30 minutes. After that, let it cool down before you whizz it in a blender (bit by bit) to make a smooth soup. When you are ready to eat, warm the soup up again in the pan.

Looking at plant products

Kinds of hardwoods and softwoods

Deciduous hardwoods

These are the trees that lose their leaves in winter. They generally grow in regions with **temperate** climates, including Europe, Japan, New Zealand, Chile and central USA. Examples of **deciduous** hardwoods are oak, ash, elm, beech, birch, walnut, sycamore, chestnut and lime.

Evergreen hardwoods

These are trees that keep their leaves all the year round. They generally grow more quickly than deciduous trees and to a larger size. They are usually softer and easier to work than deciduous trees. There are only two European **evergreens** – holly and laurel. Most evergreens are found in tropical or sub-tropical regions such as South America, Central America, Africa, Burma, India and the East and West Indies. Examples of evergreen hardwoods are mahogany, teak, African walnut, afrormosia, ebony and balsa.

Softwoods

These are produced by the cone-bearing (**coniferous**) trees. They are generally evergreen and have needle-like leaves. They grow in regions with cold or cool temperate climates such as Canada, Scandinavia and northern Russia. They grow much more quickly than hardwoods and are cheaper, softer and easier to work. Their seeds are held in cones. Common examples are pine, fir, spruce, larch, cedar and redwood.

Top ten!

Do you have any idea which are the most popular **fruits** and vegetables in the world? These top ten lists tell you which of these crops are grown most across the world.

Top ten world fruit crops:

1 Oranges
2 Bananas
3 Grapes
4 Apples
5 Watermelons
6 Coconuts
7 Plantains
8 Mangoes
9 Tangerines, clementines, satsumas
10 Pears

Top ten world vegetable crops:

1 Sugar cane
2 Rice
3 Wheat
4 Maize
5 Potatoes
6 Sugar beet
7 Cassava
8 Barley
9 Soya beans
10 Sweet potatoes

Cereal crops

Cereals are kinds of grasses. Important cereals include wheat, rice, corn, barley, sorghum, oats, millet and rye.

Wheat is one of the world's most important food crops. In many areas of the world, wheat appears in some form at nearly every meal. Most of these foods are made from the kernels (**seeds** or grains) of the wheat plant. The kernels are ground into flour to make breads, cakes, cookies, crackers, macaroni, spaghetti, breakfast cereals and other foods. The leading wheat-producing countries include Canada, China, France, India, Russia and the USA.

Corn (also called maize). The kernels can simply be cooked and eaten, but they are also used to make breakfast cereals, baked products, salad dressings and many other foods. When people eat eggs, meat and dairy products they benefit from corn indirectly, because large amounts of corn are fed to livestock.

Rice Over half of the people in the world eat rice as the main part of their meals. Rice is usually grown in flooded fields. The water also kills weeds and other pests. Rice grows best in shallow water and thrives in many tropical areas because of the warm, wet climate. China and India grow more than half of the world's rice.

Oats are an important grain crop. Farmers grow them mainly to feed livestock, but the seeds of oat plants are **processed** and used in foods such as oatmeal, oatcakes, cookies and breakfast cereals. Oats are rich in starch and high-quality protein, and they provide a good source of **vitamin** B1. Russia is the leading oat-growing country.

Rye is a cereal grain similar to wheat and barley. The plant has slender seed spikes with long, stiff awns (beards). Rye is used to make bread and certain types of liquors. The heavy, black bread of Europe is made from rye. Rye is an important crop in the cool climates of northern Europe, Asia and North America. Russia is the world's leading rye-growing country.

Millet is an important source of food in Africa and Asia. People grind the seeds into flour for flat breads and thin, fried cakes. They also use the seeds in porridge. Millet seeds, leaves and stems can be used as livestock feed.

Sorghum is grown for its round, starchy seeds. In India, Africa and China, the grain is ground and made into pancakes or mush for food. In some countries it is used for feeding animals.

Barley is made into malt and is used in alcoholic drinks (such as beer), malted milk and flavourings. Barley flour may be used in baby cereal and in bread. Barley is also used for animal feed. Russia is the leading producer of barley.

Glossary

algae kind of plant that does not have leaves, stems, roots or flowers. We call them a kind of plant because they can use sunlight to make their own food during photosynthesis.

annual rings rings you can see when the trunk of a tree is cut down. If you count annual rings, you can find out a tree's age.

antiseptic substance that destroys or stops the growth of germs

asthma lung disease causing periods of breathlessness, wheezing and coughing

bacteria tiny organisms in the soil, water and air. Some kinds of bacteria can bring about decay in dead plants and animals.

bark tough outer skin of a tree

biodegradable having the capacity to rot away in soil or sun after being thrown away. Things that are not biodegradable stay in the ground for hundreds or thousands of years, often causing pollution.

broad-leaved type of tree with flat leaves, rather than the thin needle-like leaves of conifers. Most broad-leaved trees, such as maple and oak, lose their leaves in winter.

bromeliads name for any member of a large family of tropical plants. Many are epiphytes, which grow on other plants.

bud swelling on a plant stem of tiny, young, overlapping leaves or petals and other parts of a flower, ready to burst into bloom

bulb underground bud protected by layers of thick, fleshy leaves. An onion is a kind of bulb.

calcium part of food that is vital for healthy growth, especially of the bones and teeth

carbohydrate kind of food that gives living things energy

carbon dioxide gas in the air around us that plants use for photosynthesis

cellulose substance found inside the cells of plants. It is a kind of carbohydrate and has a structure like fibre.

citrus fruits oranges, lemons, grapefruits and limes are all citrus fruits

conifer/coniferous kind of tree that has needle-like leaves and seeds that develop in cones

contaminate when something is harmed (made unhealthy) because of contact with something else

cutting part of a plant such as a leaf, stem or root that is used to make more plants

deciduous type of tree or shrub that loses all its leaves in winter

embryo a very young plant, contained in a seed

endangered species plant or animal in danger of becoming extinct (dying out)

energy ability in living things to do what they need to do in order to live and grow. Plants and animals get the energy they need from their food.

erosion process by which wind, frost and rain break rock and soil loose from one area of land and move them to another

ethanol type of alcohol obtained from plant sugars, which can be used as a fuel

evaporation when water turns from liquid into a vapour (a gas).

evergreen type of plant that does not lose all its leaves at once, but loses some leaves and grows new ones all year round

family group or type of plants

fat nutrient that gives us energy, although too much fat is bad for you. Also, energy storage material in animals.

fertilizer nutrient-rich powder or spray that plant-growers use to increase the amount or quality of their crop

fibre strand of any substance that is long and thin, like thread. We cannot digest fibres in plant parts that we eat, but as they pass through our digestive system they help to keep it healthy.

fruit part of a plant that has seeds inside. Many fruits are good to eat.

germinate when a seed starts to grow roots and shoots in the earliest stage of becoming a plant

habitat place where plants (and animals) live

hardwood another name for broad-leaved trees such as oak and maple. Hardwood trees take much longer to grow than softwood (coniferous) trees.

humid hot and wet

imported when food or goods are brought from one country to be sold in another

infection/infectious when bacteria or other germs spread from one living thing into another, and make it sick

iron mineral that is needed for healthy blood

legume family of plants including peas and beans that grow their seeds inside pods

minerals substances such as iron, which are found in some of the foods we eat, many of which are good for our health

nutrients kinds of chemicals which nourish plants and animals

oil greasy substance that does not dissolve in water. Plant oils are very useful.

organisms living things, such as bacteria, cells, plants and animals

oxygen gas in the air. Plants release oxygen into the air during the process of photosynthesis.

peat partly rotted remains of a plant called bog moss. Peat has proved to be an excellent preservative – things trapped inside peat can last a very long time without rotting away.

perennial plant that lives for more than two years, often for many years

petals coloured parts of a flower

photosynthesis process by which a plant produces its food using energy from sunlight, carbon dioxide from the air, and water from the soil

pod capsule that holds the seeds of legume plants, such as peas

pollination when pollen travels from the anthers of one flower to the stigma of the same or a different flower

pollutes/pollution when something poisons or harms any part of the environment (the natural world)

processed when plants are cooked or treated in a certain way to make a new kind of food or drink. Apples are processed to make apple juice.

protein protein is needed for growth, maintenance and repair

rainforest kind of forest that exists in very hot and wet (rainy) countries of the world

resin special kind of sticky sap that flows just beneath a tree's layer of bark

respiration process by which living things release energy from their food

roots plant parts that anchor plants firmly in the ground and take in water and nutrients

sap fluid containing food made in the leaves. Sap flows in tubes within a plant's parts, taking food from leaves to the rest of the plant.

seed seeds contain the beginnings of a new plant

shoot new stem growing from the main stem of a plant, or out of a seed

softwood another name for coniferous trees, such as pine and spruce. Softwood trees grow much more quickly than hardwood (broad-leaved) trees.

stalk long, narrow part of a plant that attaches the leaf to the stem. Flower stalks attach little flowers to a stem.

stem part of a plant that holds it upright and supports its leaves and flowers

temperate type of climate that is mild, with warmish summers and cool winters. The UK and parts of the USA have a temperate climate.

timber wood that has been cut from a tree to be used in some way

tropics area of the world around the Equator with the hottest climate in the world

trunk hard, woody stem of a tree, which is covered with bark

tuber short, thick underground stem. New tubers (and, in turn, new plants) can grow from the buds (called 'eyes') on a tuber.

vapour moisture that is suspended as droplets in air, having changed from a liquid state into a gas, like steam from a kettle

vegetarian someone who chooses not to eat meat or other products made from animals

vitamin type of nutrient in food that helps the body to grow and be protected from illness. The body needs many different types of vitamins.

wind-pollinated plants that use wind to carry their pollen from one flower to another

Find out more

Books

Eyewitness Guides: Plant and *Tree*, David Burnie, Dorling Kindersley

Eyewitness Visual Dictionaries: Plants, Deni Brown, 1992, Dorling Kindersley

Internet-linked Library of Science: World of Plants, L. Howell and K. Rogers, 2001, Usborne

Magic School Bus: Plants and Seeds, Joanna Cole and Bob Degen, 1999, Econo-clad Books

Plants, Jo Ellen Moore, 1986, Evan-Moor Educational Publishers

The Oxford Children's Encyclopedia of Plants and Animals, 2000, Oxford University Press

The Private Life of Plants, David Attenborough, 1995, BBC Books; also available as a set of videos of the BBC television series of the same name.

Websites

Great Plant Escape: fun way of learning about what different plant parts do; also a simple glossary of terms
www.urbanext.uiuc.edu/gpe/gpe.html

BBCi nature: gardening calendar, fun facts and links to Private Life of Plants information based on TV series presented by Sir David Attenborough
www.bbc.co.uk/nature/plants/

Alien explorer: looks at what plants are like and where they grow, from an outsider's point of view!
www.alienexplorer.com/ecology/topic27.html

Blooming of the titan arum: a website devoted to one of the world's most remarkable flowers – you can see its bud opening!
www.news.wisc.edu/titanarum/index.html

Habitats of the world: at Missouri Botanical Garden's website, you can compare the habitats of the world
mbgnet.mobot.org/index.htm

Conservation sites

Information on dangers to wild plants and habitats and what conservation groups are doing to help them survive

Worldwide Fund for Nature
www.wwf.org.uk

Friends of the Earth
www.foe.co.uk/campaigns/biodiversity

Eden Project: lots of information about the remarkable Eden greenhouses, where different plant habitats have been created, plus an interesting plant quiz
www.edenproject.com

Places to visit

Many museums, arboretums (botanical garden devoted to trees) and botanic gardens are fascinating places to visit. You could try:

The Royal Botanical Gardens, Kew, near London

Westonbirt Arboretum, Gloucestershire

Eden Project, St Austell, Cornwall

You can also find out about plants by visiting local garden centres.

Index

Titles in the *Life of Plants* series include:

Hardback   0 431 11883 3

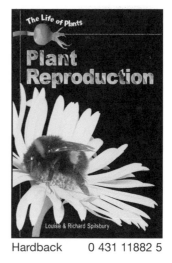

Hardback   0 431 11881 7

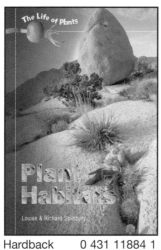

Hardback   0 431 11884 1

Hardback   0 431 11880 9

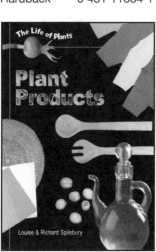

Hardback   0 431 11885 X

Hardback   0 431 11882 5

Find out about the other titles in this series on our website www.heinemann.co.uk/library